Becoming Human

Becoming Human

New Poems

Lance Lee

Authors Choice Press
San Jose New York Lincoln Shanghai

Becoming Human
New Poems

All Rights Reserved © 2001 by Lance Lee

No part of this book may be reproduced or transmitted in any form or by any means, graphic, electronic, or mechanical, including photocopying, recording, taping, or by any information storage or retrieval system, without the permission in writing from the publisher.

Authors Choice Press
an imprint of iUniverse.com, Inc.

For information address:
iUniverse.com, Inc.
5220 S 16th, Ste. 200
Lincoln, NE 68512
www.iuniverse.com

ISBN: 0-595-18878-8

Printed in the United States of America

PREVIOUS BOOKS

Poetry

WRESTLING WITH THE ANGEL

Plays

TIME'S UP AND OTHER PLAYS

TIME'S UP

FOX, HOUND & HUNTRESS
in Vol. 10, PLAYWRIGHTS FOR TOMORROW

Fiction

SECOND CHANCES

Non-Fiction

A POETICS FOR SCREENWRITERS

THE UNDERSTRUCTURE OF WRITING FOR FILM
AND TELEVISION
(WITH BEN BRADY)

Acknowledgements

Almost all of these poems have previously appeared in the United Kingdom often in multiple issues of *Acumen, Agenda, Ambit, Iron, The North, Orbis, Outposts, Pennine Platform, Poetry Nottingham, Psychopoetica, Scintilla, Seam, STAND, and Staple.*

Special thanks go to *Ambit* for first publishing the "Dante in Los Angeles" sequence, and to *Agenda* for featuring "Why The Woman Lighthouse Keeper Stays…"

Publications in the United States have included *Antioch Review, Nimrod, The Cape Rock, Connecticut River Review, Amelia 25, Blue Unicorn, POEM, and Solo 2.*

"Bats" appeared in an earlier version in **Wrestling With The Angel**.

Portrait used by permission of Ron Sandford
Cover Photo by Lance Lee

To Jeanne

Life is not a stroll across a field.

Pasternak, *Hamlet*

Contents

BECOMING HUMAN	1
RISING FAIRE	2
THE WOLF	3
1	3
2	4
3	5
SLEDDING TIME IN CARL SCHURZ PARK	6
POKER-FACED	8
THE GHOST	9
SLEEPWALKING AT DAWN	11
OUR GREAT LONELINESS	12
DANTE IN LOS ANGELES	13
I MARBLE	15
II SEA STONE	18
III SCENES FROM A MOVIE	20
IV EXILE	24
A Word of Explanation	27
PERFORMING IN LONDON	28
BATS	29
BEACHED LIKE A WHALE	31
RUNNING WITH THOREAU	32
KILLERS	35
FOR SOMETHING IN THE WORLD DOES NOT LIKE US*	38
CHARTRES	39
THE LIGHT AT VEZELAY	40
CATHEDRAL, AND EVENSONG	41
THE ABSENCE OF GOD	43
ALL I AM	44
IN THE EYE OF THE STORM	45
A GREY WIND IN NANTUCKET	46
WINTER LESSONS IN LOS ANGELES	48
EL NIÑO	49

TREES IN DECEMBER	50
THE WHEATFIELD	52
WHAT WE HAVE TO DO	53
TOTEM	54
RAVENS	56
THE DEER	57
GEESE	58
WHAT GOD DOES WITH OWLS	60
PERRY MILL POND	62
AN OLD BARN IN WESTON	63
ANGELS	64
BORDER CROSSING	65
MADONNAS AND OTHER STRANGERS	67
PIAF SINGS	69
VENUS AT VERDUN	70
DRIVING INTO ITALY	72
RAPALLO	74
THE LIGHT AT RAPALLO	76
DACHAU	78
HISTORY	80
END OF THE CENTURY	82
THE QUAKER GRAVEYARD IN NANTUCKET	83
WHY THE WOMAN LIGHTHOUSE KEEPER…	86
1	86
2	87
3	88
THE FRUIT TREES AT GUNNERSBURY CEMETERY	90
DUST	94
INNOCENCE	99
WOLF WIND	101
THE SOUTH SUSSEX DOWNS	102

BECOMING HUMAN

The dog's tail pounds the crib's bars,
black and ominous, waking me—
or the moans do from the nearby bed
where my parents couple. Slowly
my eyes move up the wall,
but where the ceiling should enfold,
star beyond star pulls me deeply
into the night. Fear swells,
and my heart throbs—I gulp the
breathless vacuum, and thrash—
then wake, swallowing
great gulfs of air like milk.
Slowly night spins down
and topples over.... I see the terror
that fills my heart so suddenly, so often,
is just the memory dreamed here
of how I learned I was alone
and became human. That terror lies
at the root, nutriment and gnawing tooth:
it is the life I must not wake from, now.

RISING FAIRE

Just this phrase glimpsed from an old book:
'rising faire,' the gothic 's' an 'f' shape:
nothing more. I grieve when grief
is done, give thanks
once the moment has passed, armored
against all current passion,
not rising faire, but before, or after.

That 'rising faire' betrays an innocent
joy in life, the mirror to see
present impairment by.
It's the state every child knows
daily rising faire to eternity:
I knew it then.
Lament with me,

or dream of rising faire again
to faith undamaged, love uncompromised
and requited: to the life
we let slip away, much as a child
who leaves his yard for the beckoning woods
loses his way
long before he thinks to stop.

THE WOLF

1

A wolf lived beneath the stairs:
when I ran across the living room
his breath singed my legs before
I leaped to the safety of the steps.
I was four, the year they told me
I had one mother, not two:
the year my sister was born and
bemedalled Uncle came home
and barred me from his mother's room
as father had already from mine.
I listened to Prokofiev's story
about the boy who cried wolf too often,
and thought, alone at night
despite those softnesses just down
the hall that teased my mind,
he has nothing on me
with my own wolf at my heels…

2

An early TV stood before his lair,
screening him with images.
I remember one, a white horse
at war's end, legs splayed
topsy-turvy in tattered snow,
staring back in fear like me
whenever I crossed that room...
The house felt frozen yet feral,
springing again and again
from some deep trance
as Mother, Father, Grandmother, Uncle
smiled and smiled and smiled
over girlfriends, infidelities, rivalries.
Snowy images lingered on those early TVs
from Father Knows Best, or I Remember
    Mama,
and all the other waking lies we echoed
as though the black true beast was not
the dark screen our family idyll
    glimmered on.
That was the war to me, not the
wide, slaughtered starving world.

3

Grandmother sold that house
to stop our warring masteries.
I thought then to cross rooms wide as years
    without pursuit:
that such hunger I felt, desire
turning on itself, anger
the world could never match a boy's dream
were just my childhood lot. But now
I am in the middle wood, winding
    in the trees,
hurrying through the clearings, I know
the rage desire and anger feed and form
    is not put by—
for the wolf runs in the heart:
there is nowhere to hide.

SLEDDING TIME IN CARL SCHURZ PARK

The hill lays prostrate in the heat,
this barely tilted, dreaded ground
I watch myself pellmell down
in winter, age eight, hands frozen

on the sled's handles with fear and
courage, all as though filmed in old
super eight.
      Or strange boys and I play
cowboy and Indian by this deserted tree

in one of those descents to disaster
I sometimes will—frames speed by
while they tie me to the trunk and steal
my new guns, running off laughing:

I sweat shame and twist free, then
walk home like this tree has grown,
close to the ground as an old man.
In one reel Grandmother sits between

a woman airing her geranium and a
man with a snake in a bag—and holds
Oscar on a string, the big box turtle
I free next week. This blooming garden

is bordered by paths that step in broad
curves to the East River Promenade—
this little plot, those few steps at war
with their vast sweep in memory,

so much less now because
I have lost childhood's greatness.
Even so I know time is more
than stony markers: it is these films

we run back and forth at once—
just now I grasp my sled's handles
and launch down the freezing slope:
the hill unspools like film unwound,

snow falls, and night reaches for me,
my face red from snowmelt, gleaming,
young, not yet trained to march
lockstep by step to my own decline.

POKER-FACED

Was I twelve? I had just lied to father—
mother challenged me later as we waited
at a light and the 3rd. Avenue El shook
overhead, not to say I had done wrong
but ask how I did so well. Some truth

had to be withheld from father's unreason,
and my success, cool, calculating, adult,
made mother think me now a full ally.
She sensed this outfacing a parent

was my changeling moment, not some
accomplishment flung proudly at their feet
but the daily deceits by which the family
now survived made sinew and self.
I was cool, unflinching with her too, and

wondered what secrets might now be shared:
surely I could cut father down farther:
this was better than our Sunday war games
when we fought with lead soldiers he

delighted in, but victory was unsure.
But she turned away. I think she saw herself
mirrored, and felt a little horror
at how cheaply and with what pleasure
I flung boyhood and innocence away.

THE GHOST

billows in full sunlight beside
the overturned chaise lounge, feet floating
over the lawn, rainsoaked rhododendron
blooms glimpsed through her dress
as purple stains. I guess

she's my young grandmother or
my mother's loose-haired loose-
clothed dream of herself one summer day
before her life settled in
come to judge me—or

my middle-aged hunger for beauty
come to taunt with what cannot be.
I'm hungry for her to forgive me
but when I read my strangeness
in her eyes, I feel

a stone settle on my shoulders
for each compromised year and know
she is the measure of my fading.
She leaves like a photo brightening to white
I race to fill in with features

of everyone I have known—and I sense
I am wrong, that she would let all of us
touch the blood of our births
to lip and tongue and again
be young, if she could. I float

over the damp grass after her like a double
exposure looking to merge with its original
until harsh with this giddiness
I pull back to the first moment
I saw her so troubled to be seen by me:

she knew then I would follow
no better angel into a second life
but locked in stubborn flesh and decay,
inevitably betray what all men do:
life, love, eternal youth.

SLEEPWALKING AT DAWN

This light gives the luster of pale flesh
to the ocean, or pearls into the still waves
of the hills. Ghosts haunt this edge
between the two certainties, dark or bright—
dream-cum-memories walk abroad,
their shadows balm on the raw heart.

They assume the faces we mourn, even
the child's who runs in the unlit blood
shouting my name. No one is lost, they say.
Shameless with joy I float uphill in the
stillness, or wing downward in lazy circles
over the water with those thoughtless
I never thought would be in my company
held in the round O of my arms, for I know
a honed orange blade will shear hill from sky,
land from water, living from dead easily
as a bomb exploding in the heart:
and that I will waken into myself, then,
and resume the poverty of my forgetting.

OUR GREAT LONELINESS

Sweet Rosemary, fresh as new snow,
white skin ablush from fun as we played
on the top bunk... Not children, not teens,
we kept our eyes on the game though I
saw the clean line of her thighs
her skirt half hid, and felt such desire
I saw myself push the game aside
and cover her face with kisses,
then cover her as a man a woman,
cries of ecstasy filling my ears.
I thought she must see, and recoil,
but she played on, oblivious, or pretended
to see and feel nothing of my wild want...
I felt alone, and untrue, and ached.

I return to this moment often—
a silver brooch still holds her hair,
and her scent envelops me as we bend
our heads so our breathing blends,
yet never, then or later, more... Always
I wonder at our silence, and feel
manhood and childhood begin to part
as the first mature touch of that great
loneliness a man and woman shares
brushes my heart.

Dante in Los Angeles
four imitations after Dante

I MARBLE

after Dante's *Io son venuto*

When December strings Orion
in the canyons' throats, and touches
their summits with rare snow, Saturn
glitters like sunlit ice and Venus
vanishes in daylight. Then I might tell stories
of a doomed hunter, a god of a golden age,
or a goddess surfing on dawn's foam,
but in Hubble's universe tireless stars race
from each other through endless winter,
and skies full of metal spies hold no epics
or romances. So I chase without pause
in this woman's wake who is colder
than an airless rock in space.

More often we burn in false summers
when winter winds press through our
canyons from the desert; or Mexican
rains drift north and drench us warmly
until a storm from Alaska rolls
down the green wave of the coast
to clear the air with almost frozen rain
and dress our mountains in white.
Such tumults should distract me from
my private Monroe or Harlow or Stone,
but hot cold wet arid, these polar reversals
echo my own moods as I pursue this woman
who doesn't care if I am false or true.

Now cedar waxwings, starlings and
swallows have flown, and fluttering,

gaudily orange monarchs. Cats
that howl and mate all summer
silently stalk abandoned yards:
bulls in our mountain ranches
dream below sycamore and alder. I envy
their great mass of muscle, dull mind,
treetrunk limbs—no girl-cum-woman
weighs them down with constant denials.
Age grows heavy on my shoulders
as in greener times those bulls
on cows they mount, bellowing.

Yet narcissus blooms by Christmas,
then violets stain the garden blue:
ocampus leaves I cut to the ground
grow large as elephant ears… By February
white flowers dot the plum's bare limbs,
and tulips part resisting earth as they
spear upward from their bulbs—
sex is always rampant, here… Look at me,
lusting for this young thing though
she shoves me aside the way
soft shoots crack and move concrete.
This must be hell, I think, in constant fear
some other will see her bud and open.

Too much or too little tells our story—
the creeks run dry, or rampage
as hills too full of rain fall to the flood
bubbling over rock and log as though gas
exploding from some deep earthquake-
opened rift: bridges and homes, dams,
and plows meant to shore hasty levees
are all swept out to sea. And when, later,

the scum of standing pools turns green
as corroded copper, I am no better off,
but still chase her with a lethal happiness,
starting to love what I hate—shame, and
suicidal thoughts my helplessness awakes.

What will happen if she stays as hard
when mockingbirds come home and sing
every love song they know all night long,
dancing in the trees' dark leaves?
I'll hold her in my heart anyway, and turn
by inches into what I want, as all men do,
even if that means growing marble-hearted, too.

II SEA STONE

after Dante's *Al poco giorno*

This woman is a stone, a whitening of grass,
a day circling into shadow, a cold that burns:

even so
my hunger stays green in her white hills

whose hardness belies her beauty.
When the year turns and hills burn green and
    flower,

I cling to her heels like a shadow
though she stays cold as snow in shade:

when she garlands her hair with laurel and ivy,
I am bound to her hard flesh more than a stone set
    in cement—

and when she dresses in green, so lovely, so lying,
I crawl after her, chewing the grass she walks on

though I am touched by gray and know better.
She turns the shade of trees to asphalt that burns and
    cracks from cold,

the grave to remembered misery without release—
even dust forgets its hunger for life in her shadow.

I would eat through her dry hills if a river,
wear shale into sand, make her flower:

or slice her foot if a sharp flint hidden in grass
mingling blood with garlands torn from her hair
    in pain.

That might not change her nature, but I would be
    glad,
for she is a stone made in darkness and cold and
    crushing weight

I cannot take from my heart
however she weighs me down and makes me old.

III SCENES FROM A MOVIE

after Dante's *Cosi nel mio*

Pursuit

Others envy me on the street
with this young woman on my arm,
but she goes no farther, thwarting
my experience and desire.
I crave her as a man does
afraid his passion is his last,
shamefully stringing myself along
although I should forget her.
She seems slight, but every word
tells me this woman is a killer
who never needs to say *No*
but lets me stay because she knows
I know how little she cares.

Montage

My mind flowers on the stalk
she holds in marble hands.
Or I am the ocean's flat plate
she crosses bored, untossed.
She is a rasp, and my soul
the wood or steel she grates:
or she gnaws on my heart
as though on the treat
a rat threads its maze towards.
Every woman I have loved

and let go adds to her power,
especially those who were better:
Not this time, I swear, and am lost.

Exposed

Alone, anguish is the monkey
driving me down the street
where I shout her name
like a homeless person delusion-
hagged, oblivious, only afraid
she will see me and laugh.
Here's a duel well past obsession!
I thought those stories romances
that make love a primal power
stronger than mind and will—
but look at me now, a man
who goes on loving a woman
who chooses to be cruel.

Committed *

Again and again I raise my hand
against myself—this straitjacket
pins my arms—the movement
is in my mind: I am not well.
I butt against a padded wall,
cry, no yell, until hoarse, still
not believing I'm here as blood
rushes to my heart and leaves me
white, swollen, enraged, faint.
I split apart and hit myself so hard
another blow from this familiar
stranger will kill. Yes, yes I know

this is just ingrown, rejected passion—

**

if only I could let loose on her!
But she breaks me apart
in daylight or shade, at dawn
or twilight, assassin, robber, this
dove hard as a diamond!
I'm in a hot, close place and howl,
hungry to hear her yowl, too—
and if she did, would forgive her
all. Then I would play with
her blonde hair and whisper
I'll help you, knowing
surprised by such kindness
she might start to love.

Dream

Her hair whips my face, my chest…
I grab and urge her on all
one afternoon and evening
with bearish caresses, consumed
with revenge but never hurting.
I just tease, sure, full of menace,
staring into those jasper eyes
that make my blood hot as lava
pouring through green shade.
She may be slow to kindle,
but once the damage she's done
burns her to a guilty response,
we live through tumults of peace.

Release

Woman, I give you up but don't
let go, waiting to see you treated
the same. Revenge? I am the image
of your neglect and live in winter,
old and small and bitter.

IV EXILE

    after Dante's *Amor, da che convien*

What brute, possessive power
  drives me after this woman
      beautiful as rainfall sparkling
from a bright, clear sky?
  Who cold-shoulders love aside
      no matter what I do
or how my failures
  estrange me from my self?
      She floats overhead at night
and robs me of sleep:
  it's shameful
      how my body hardens and
my breath grows short
  as though she is there—
      no wonder I shout

in the house, on the street,
  ready to pin back anyone's ears
      who will listen,
a middle-aged man who jumps
  through any hoop malice
      puts in her hands.
I'm crying, see,
  but not from grief—
      opening her locked door
would make me whole,
  but passion rides me
      like a tree the wind
blows hard enough to break:
  as dead wood snaps off, the new

    takes the wind's shape.

Friends, I'm in trouble:
  her image is so alive
      in my mind, it drives
after the woman it's modeled on:
  I follow like a prisoner
      crazy enough to run
towards execution,
  futile as snow
      falling on the sun.
She is there too,
  and watches unmoved
      as a uniformed thug
makes me kneel and
  bends my head
      and cocks his gun…

So I learn to walk dead
  in sense, spirit or soul,
      morally dead, not mad,
driven to learn how
  a man goes outwardly on
      while ridden by a force
our words and tepid lives
  we think we regret
      have lost expression for.
Animal and cunning,
  I would wallow in coarse
      frank sex to win her,
or be pure as black light
  however she strips me to my
      subhuman raw.

Even this river that flows
   past the childhood home
      I left, never dreaming,
uprooted, I would be
   a stranger everywhere,
      leaves me inconsolable.
Along the banks, raspberries
   open white flowers,
      and barely unfurled leaves
mottle the bare limbs' brown
   while she holds me encased
      in polar ice…
And if I could come home,
   be at peace, and always warm,
      I know what I would say:

my heart is sore from her denials;
   let no man say he aches more:
      yet I will stay if she relents,
unrepentant by her side
   a stranger to everything but
      my own exiling love.

A Word of Explanation

These are very free versions of poems found in Dante's collected lyrics, the **Rime**. The first three are drawn from the Pietra series of impassioned but flinty love poems Dante wrote to a young, unresponsive woman in his maturity. The woman is never named beyond being called a stone in one way or another, and is unknown. The impact of her refusal provoked a psychologically realistic response in Dante new in a medieval poet and unlikely to be expressed absent real experience. *EXILE* is based on *Amor, da che convien*, the last of the poems gathered in the **Rime**. It is not one of the Pietra poems, and not addressed to the same young, rejecting woman, although akin in sentiment. I would like to think these versions give a taste of the poems as they might have been had Dante written them now, in Los Angeles.

PERFORMING IN LONDON

When the lights dim and rise the actors
withdraw from the audience into their roles,
and Petruchio and Kate renew their duel—

then I am hauled onstage to drag his father to jail,
policewoman's cap slapped on my head,
my three concubines, so named in the earlier fun,

cousin and two daughters, in helpless laughter.

Later, at Florian's, when the Grappa is done
three bottles of Italian champagne line up
waiting their cue as I devour a daffodil

peppered and dipped in olive oil, astounding
cousin Felicity and eldest, Heather:
how good these petals taste!

I am not the sober father I seemed to them, now

though renewing myself like a role on the page
given a new performance is an old device:
no wonder the English love the theatre so,

we both dive so deeply into our lives we forget
the soul delights in all the roles it can play.
It languishes, as Petruchio would, if

bound forever to one unwavering plea.

BATS

I have been troubled by bad dreams,
so when twilight floods out of things
into darkness, and my face appears
in the window when I turn on the light,
I study its broad, high cheekbones
that make the flesh photograph heavier
than it is, the straight gentile nose,
brown eyes that stare straight out, head
held high: brown hair the sun burns blonde
from the celt and german in my blood;
the familiar, ironic twist of lips.
Not much suggests the ghettos of Kiev
or Polish Vilna my father's fathers left,
or why any from those left behind
should crowd into my dreams
with my face, my pipe, book, beercan,
wallet photos, loose change in their hands
from the mass graves and lime
they must have gone into, holding air…
Their history is divorced from mine.
They never came here. They are divorced
by my father's family's rush
from Gumbinski to Levy, now Lee,
divorced once my father let my mother
raise me anglican, not jewish.
When father's father heard of that he shouted:
"Are you a mouse or a man?" at his son,
yet when grandfather died I found
Hebrew prayers for the dead
on my father's bureau: he never said them
that we could hear. 'Remember
those who were lovely in their lives

whether they were killed, slain, slaughtered
burned, drowned, or strangled:
ask for their names in your blood:
blood remembers' I say, now,
though words never saved anyone,
though I cannot imagine being led out
to a hot dissolving dark...
The wind soughs through the trees—

> *I look in the mirror—I am twenty*
> *years older than I thought. I stand up,*
> *stretch my legs, strange from the coma*
> *that held me. I walk down a street*
> *and push a Jew into the gutter:*
> *he bobs, he cringes, he snaps one look*
> *at my well-dressed pitiless shape—.*

My head snaps out of sleep. I am sore
and sweating and turn the light off.
My face vanishes. I open the window
on the night, and the wind comes in.
We always think we'll do the right thing.
Outside bats hunt down the helpless
with their sharp, black wefts of song.
I slide downwind with them, violent and small.

BEACHED LIKE A WHALE

A beached whale buffeted by
whisky and caffeine in a bar,
I quaff stray girls for chasers.
My thirst is a pit, and anger
at the man sedated by his paper
near the window. I shatter glass,
scatter pretzels and peanuts
across the floor. They soothe me
swiftly as my two mothers would
when deep pangs beached me
in an alien air where all
we did grew strange.
These here now hope I will
strangle in my own bulk—
but I am swimming, all are
swimming in a breathless deep
searching for our image in
another's eyes to be sure
we are not alone, for I fear
this freedom I seek
expresses only the solitude
built in the bone. I heave
out the door, leaving, as ever,
chaos in my wake. I feel such
hunger that even when full
I am hollow, and ache.

RUNNING WITH THOREAU

Strange hungers drive him
through Walden's oaks and pines
after vole or fox or deer,
longing to gulp hot blood
and still fluent muscle,

face red, eyes shining
even as ferocity pulls him
to all fours, then to his belly
where he twists side to side
and coils, hissing.

At first light he finds
his cabin door and crosses
the threshold, shaken, human.
Later he floats on the pond
feeling disembodied as his face

stares back from the surface
mingled with clouds,
for he knows now
what thrives in the blood
is "sensuous" and "reptile".

I know him well
in this land where I
listen to coyotes sing
on the near ridge at night
and imagine them hunting

through dense growth—
then hear Thoreau
running in the canyon woods
and slide beside him,
my snout tugged forward

as I topple to my paws,
canines thrusting from my jaw,
symphonies of spoors
growing vivid on my tongue
as we hunt swiftly over

the forest's rotting floor.
That feral nature I
always knew was mine
overwhelms my heart—
until I find a familiar door

and hesitate, listening
on the threshold
for my wife's breathing inside.
I remember how it was
when children lived here,

and how we made love
when they slept, laughing
as we swallowed our cries.
I straighten to full height,
wondering

why our hands
are not all stained red
by the animal we are.
Nights pass, months, years
as the answer grows,

yet even now when
blood cries for blood,
I barely know how to guard
the small exchanges of love
that make me a man.

KILLERS

I stop by a hillside
    where thrashers scream
        and squirrels chur alarms
leaping for steep burrows,
        all but one
    a black flash takes by the throat.
    The squirrel flails,
but the cat chokes off its cries,
    then backs into the chaparral
        to avoid clods I heave—
I know food waits for him,
    sunning on some floor:
        he kills without need.

But before he disappears
    a coyote leaps from cover—
        a quick back and forth snap
of the cat's neck stops its cries.
    Then the bent U
        of a puma springs open:
one hard whack crumples the canine,
    yelping.
        Finally I pounce,
        caught up in this river of fantasy,
the white sun of my gun
    bursting
        in the lion's eyes…

I shake my head at the pleasure
    this carnage brings
        then suddenly wonder,
How much more would I feel

if I killed men?
          Free of instinct,
      everything chance,
what bars me from murder?
      Would I feel revulsion
          brushing a death camp's fatty ashes
from my sleeve?

exploding a plane to rain bodies
      from the sky?
          mowing men down
as though painted targets at a fair?
      Or would the crimes' size and thrill
          make me feel powerful?
feel I cleanse my ugliness
      by calling others ugly
          and killing that with them?
feel such deaths become
      primal offerings in my stead
          to gods with bloody lips?

Or would I just go home
      from a killing field
          soaked to my knees in blood,
sunset a body swiftly turning
      hard and black,
          and once there
smile at my wife and child
      as they cook and play and,
          while I stare down the empty O
of the gunbarrel I clean,
      feel—
          nothing?
      Men do all these. I am a man.

The sun is heavy on my head,
    pinning me like a wrestler
        to the ground.
Even the tortured cries of thrashers
    are still in this light.
        Pungent smells war in the heat—
wild sage, chamise and toyon,
    monkey flower, mountain lilac:
        there's no clean balance in nature,
no peace not a sleeping violence.

I would like to pretend, oh
    any nature but this,
but all I have is this hard honesty,
    a chalice whose stones are gone,
        whose sheen is beaten off,
full of mere breath, my life
    so mercifully spared
        the easy deaths in my heart.

FOR SOMETHING IN THE WORLD DOES NOT LIKE US*

Damn these roses! they cede flowers
in ones and twos on threadbare stalks—
for all love's wasted water, they are piles
of shattered axles scavenged from derelict cars.

But when night snuffs the moon and stars
these roses unfold abundant leaves and blooms
whose ripe scent makes the air dense with yearning:
now opossum surrenders stealth to startled passion,
and mouse in owl's grasp feels less pain than ecstasy
as talons tighten and the beak descends.

Damn these roses! At dawn
their rich profusion withdraws
and the sharp, rust-colored piles speak
of the danger that shears our beauty, if bared,
with the lie we bloom from pain and loss
instead of overflowing life, and love, and joy.

That is the shadow that haunts our hearts
and makes us sweat in the dark,
for we are not innocent—look
what blades my hands become
when someone flowers in front of me,
even my own self I can barely stop from cutting down.

*after Thoreau on Mt. Ktahdin

CHARTRES

Lioness, you crouch on your hill,
poised above Beauce's rolling plains.
The Euer slips by at your feet; countless
bright eyes roll over its bridges
through long winter nights.

You crouch, not soar, though low
town roofs still come no higher
than your knees, and the odd
mispaired steeples dominate
as when gaudy nobles passed
and near slaves toiled in the fields.

How much faith, disease, mindful
violence, wealth and poverty
shaped your stony sinews?
Golden in late light or iron in grey,
chilled in the bone summer or winter,

indifferent crowds routinely pick
pelt and claw, unaware how
you wait for those hungry
with your hunger to enter,
to be eaten whole by faith,
to cease to be, to become another's.

                                                    Chartres, 1995

THE LIGHT AT VEZELAY

This light pours pure as clear water
through La Madeleine's plain windows,
laving the woman's relics who loved
too well yet was greeted first by Christ
when he returned from hell.

Once knights jumbled downhill
colorful as tumbled tourist curios
as St. Bernard called for a new crusade:
when they roared consent,
birds fell from flight, stunned.

Now we enjoy pastoral views,
then stop for tea and pastries, girls
in starched aprons, no one about
this Sunday in November but us
as sunset flushes walls and roofs

deeply as ingenues with lovers.
But I cannot kneel and pray
in this sore and dreamless time
however I feel the old hunger
for something better in my heart,

for this light falls always on hungry flesh
and world-weary pilgrim, saint, and
soldier cutting his way to victory
with a prayer: even now, somewhere,
it imbues the blood of innocents

with a bright, deranging beauty.

CATHEDRAL, AND EVENSONG

Denim-feathered, homeless flocks scatter
and resettle, smoldering, as I enter Wren's
    stony order
cluttered with the marbled dead.
                              Evensong's
vowels swoop and swallow under his dome—

    He, remembering his mercy...
    hath scattered the proud
    in the imagination of their hearts...
    His mercy is on them that fear...

I kneel, though a stranger and doubter
as my million-yeared forbear stirs in my blood
who shed instinct and fur when he
raised the first thighbone with the first

triumphant cry over some cracked skull,
some fanged enemy's,
        or some kin's,
and seeded my blood with that need to atone
that temples my chaos with its poor beauty.

The service beats against me, longing
for an end to God's wrath, or our own
turning inward against our sins,
but only my wanting to be touched touches me,

and the failure of beauty to be the truth, or even,
    enough,
for I am one of those homeless
primed for mayhem and remorse,
and my spirit calls nowhere home.

My knees are stiff as I shamble from the nave.
Outside, the peace of afternoon falls on me
like leaves in a walk through autumn woods
as the sky mops its blue dome under the last blaze
    of light;

the peace of evening rustles from the shadows
like a cornfield's tassels in the wind
or the silks on a girl's thighs I have longed for,
alive and numb with passion, doubting she
    would come—

but what creeps from the crypt at night
is marble quaking into flesh
to haunt hearts like my own,
half soft, half stone.

                            St. Paul's, London, 1993

THE ABSENCE OF GOD

Light falls on the floor
crisp as a cracker. Even
indoors my breath fogs—
I have broken the walls
between out there and here.
Ruffles of wind blow
where there were windows:
leaves rustle all night
across my bed, and
like dew, starlight gathers
on my shoulders: because
I say my thoughts uncensored
I live alone, but not empty.
Look at this light!
It is all I have—
when it rains, the rain
is all I have—if god
talked to me, his words
would be all I have
just as now, in deep silence,
his absence is all I have. Bare
as a white bone on a
windraked shore, I am filled
with cleanliness.

ALL I AM

Start with stone, or damp earth
and bare flesh; with a sky
scraped sere, and blazing, or filled
with soft tumults—not the vast cities
that darken my mind and confuse
a flesh made for another life,
human among all inhuman others.
Start with bones in the desert
or in leaf mold in the forest
where rot and renewal are one event:
leave the airwave patter
that makes me bloodless and mad,
and the urban drone
gunshots and arson leaven,
and be alone and strange
in an empty, natural place.
Dip my arms in cold stream water
or flee from lightning-sparked fire,
a sensible panic in my mind…
Run past need, run for the sheer pleasure
of flight muscled by my own feet,
               run
until seared lungs make me stop.
One gasp runs into another—
breathe—die—breathe—die—breathe—
               there—
that is all I am, a breath…

IN THE EYE OF THE STORM

The roofs steam and the steam blurs
into silver air that burns my eyes:
only the dark screen of the avocado tree
makes the steam visible, aswirl
as thin silk on dancing limbs.

Yet if one bright day followed another
beauty would blur to boredom
and my heart grow ripe as an avocado
too long on the branch,
and yearn for downward flight.

The torrents renew, and spring
in great watery arcs and spouts
from the roofs. I am released but chastened,
for where is that vital balance
where I may know myself, and live?

> *Between the earthbound seed and the*
> *white sun burning down, desire and*
> *ripeness, the clear day and storm; between*
> *the heart whose redness no one living sees, and*
> *that death whose husk I split again and again.*

A GREY WIND IN NANTUCKET

All last night the grey wind blew
from Madaket past moor and Sconset bluffs
into the steep Atlantic: blew
past this high room only a step from cloud
and the road where wind always blows
and so seems always in the same place,
restless as me. Moments ago
our love cries floated outside
just as captain and maidservants'
fell with the lightness of scented pollen
from a high room of our friends' house
across the way long years ago.
No one disturbed them then, or us, now,
though that captain's wife listened
for the lovers' footsteps to descend.
She said nothing when they appeared,
to preserve their lie: now she haunts
    the wooden passageways,
no more able to rest than old harpoon and
    hook in the attic
who dream of green sea pastures turned red
from whale-bread sliced at its harvest.
That grey wind blew as our friends
shared family woes, always so unique
    and so alike,
born from love from truth from kin
who do what they must which we must endure
with a growing knowledge of evil, the grey wind
    knows,
blow by blow.
        Our curtains hang still:
the slow front that pummeled our thin roof

and woke me early, sags eastward.
Light so drenches the room
only kindnesses seem possible.
I don't know what our friends will do,
but love, turn to me again here, for we are in
some grace of tide and sun-shattered storm,
free to fill these moments with our joy
before the grey wind returns
and we too must wait,
like that listening wife, caught
in some enduring knot of yearning,
for lost happiness.

WINTER LESSONS IN LOS ANGELES

Winter's thirtieth day is the same
as autumn, all desert winds
flicking red tongues on the seaward sky,
blackened lemons and persimmons
dried months ago rattling on their limbs.
I still have no will to summon,
but lie on the lawn, scorched leaves
blowing over my face.
Starlings and thrushes exchange
choruses from the high eucalyptus
where they pause in passage
to and fro Mexico, uncertain
which way to go. Even death wanders dazed
as rhododendron blooms blend
last year with next,
and January's tomatoes ripen
above December's mulch. Violets
burn across the seared lawn
and the gladioli spear through old stalks
that had no time to fall.
There is no cold to give the heart
pause, no rain, yet all things grow,
feeding on themselves. By now
I should know felicity must be wrung
from warring urges; that I am
a single root for ending and beginning—
but I am slow to accept I am
both the tree dark birds leave,
and their wings forever going home
when home is always somewhere else,
tomorrow.

EL NIÑO

They say *El Niño is coming*, warm water rising in an arc
    between Asia and South America.
They say it will fatten storms like bears cuffing salmon
    from rivers.
They say we must seal, tar, shingle, or sheathe our homes
    in plastic:
the great wave of land will roll back from its rush upshore,
    bury roads in its ebb, turn the ocean brown.
How vivid their voices are now some great upheaval
    promises to match and solace their hearts' emptiness
    and ache.
They say *We must live differently, we must love differently,*
we must die differently.
Our peace is broken, we see peace was always a lie: come, violence;
    strip us with streaming waters, let suffering make us rich.
But why '*El Niño*', little one, child, if not from some blind
    impulse to honor our youth
whose innocence was our necessary victim? We read our hearts
    in signs flashing across the sky,
in strangers who parade our own desires, in odd turns of
    common things, in weather, in storms…
I say *El Niño is returning* across the dark river where we banish
    our losses;
he is nemesis and relief, baptism, last rite, exorcism and
    atonement,
certain we will always owe more than we can pay, and right.

TREES IN DECEMBER

Now trees come into their own
discarding summer's disguises:
their bared limbs may be leaden
under grey skies, but when they burn
silver in the clear light after storms
I see, astonished, a tree
is more brilliant than I.

When they pull on the tight
sleeves of winter ice they become
dynamos of color at dawn, flashing
as the sun barely tops their crowns

while I am heavy clay with no
reverent gleam of autumn leaves
at my feet. I thought to judge,
but I am judged instead
by these bright realities…
I will root into the earth and lift
skyward from one settled place,

burn and freeze
a turbine of prisms,
a company of gnarled fists,
and let life flash free, and fade, and fall
     and flash again

like the quick wings of nuthatch and
linnet, jay and cardinal in flames
beside the dull ember of his wife.
They exult in my strong nakedness,
in my taut arms and torso,
in the carefree way I shed the years
less settled lives chase and flee.

THE WHEATFIELD

I hum like a dynamo, tense
with power. Ripeness swells
up my stalks and seedheads
throb under a high hot sun,
unsure whether to burst or melt.
All is alive as a woman about to bear,
near fields bellied as seaswells
that dive below each other
as continents do when they meet.
I long for the scythe to end
this choking fullness, to be
stubble, and bare, and feel
autumn's seawind, cool and salt,
on my stripped earth—and then
in the late year be plowed while
the gulls' white leaves cloud the sky
behind the farmer's furrowing.
Brown earth, cold cast seed
firing slowly towards the root—
joy is not peace or summer's gold
but this swinging between barren and bursting poles
that makes me complete.

WHAT WE HAVE TO DO

There are bluebirds here, sparkling on the ground;
along the bank fernheads unroll in clear light.
My face looks up at me from the still pool
    where the day moon floats:
above the valley, thunderheads thrust their bellies
    on the peaks,

while lightning avidly tongues the canyons.
These are the silent thunder in every chest,
the pulses sparking nerve to nerve,
the quiet self unfolding, or rampant with hunger.

Later, the middle air dissolves the storms.
A campfire, friends, words warm as coals.
Tomorrow I return to things and things and more things
and to the daily body count from the streets.

It's hard to make myself look beyond
the greed and menace drumming in the blood,
and easy to turn my back on men and fail
to try and focus beyond the embers' glow

our rapacious, dreaming, bloody-handed soul.

TOTEM

A great bear dwells in himself
a bee sinking in his own honey.
He's white as I am under his fur,
a greater man made bearable by disguise.
He's my familiar stranger, shadowing my dreams,
linking my troubled mind to its animal core,
now pulling me blindly into the orbit of his danger,
tree-scaler,
    log-smasher,
        man-mauler,
            so sure
of himself he ignores my approach.
Heat coils in his fur invisibly as flame in sunlight;
shimmers, as if a mirage, dissolving yet
    solid:
    but when he stirs
a single wave of motion breaks to its feet—
then he circles me until
his breath blurs with mine, until
his fur grows outward from my skin—

    ah...

How loose this heavy hide, how delicious
    this heat burning inward,
refining my mind to an undivided whole
still and focused as a brilliant coal.
Now the bees flee before us, showing the way
to their honey...
        Such easy power,
mad swarming
    sweetness

    and stings:
such wild freedom growing, growing in my heart.

RAVENS

glide through winter trees, black wings gorgeous
and sober, more emblem than animal. They trail
the silence of remembered thunder,
long, slanting sheets of hail,
snow, braising our eyes, wind
sharp as a blade stropped back and forth on skin.

I glide with them as the white world unscrolls below
in words so familiar they go unread
until a soft breast turning hard
sets a cold and carrion joy clicking in my head…
There's something savage in my heart,
and something more, something twofold in the red
  world

the muscles, imbued, enfold; the enigma
as old as spirit versus flesh,
the trapped incandescence
shining beyond the gore
that sets me free from the gathering wings
swooping to their prey in the cold…

Grace lives on such a narrow, hard-to-hold margin.
I turn home to where my loved ones wait
with their dreams and innocence,
never thinking of what passes in the woods
or of how swiftly this sky darkens and becomes
all black wings and whitened eyes.

THE DEER

pauses in driving rain where eucalyptus husks
feather the wet ground, bright as stars:
one moment only our eyes meet—an ear flicks—
then he leaves before he turns away.

I think even death must come and go this way.
No wonder blood and bone honor the hunger
to make a work like a hand painted on stone
that says
    Look! I was here!
           But I prefer

this raw wind to blow through my mind,
this meeting of animal and man
that reminds me I was once within the landscape,
not the viewer I have become,

though what is my life but a swift passage, you
a chance meeting, a pause, a stare, a sharing
blood tingling—
        then separation falling between us
like the dark pour of the woods?

However I puzzle, what go on are
this fresh tang, the stars I walk on as I go,
clouds racing, rain, and somewhere out there,
another always at home.

GEESE

Daily they practice flights of Vs
these buoy shaped birds
who soon must fly south.
The sky whitens with the season,
frost burns the tundra gold and red:

one day ice shines through noon
and hearts harden to the gauntlet
they must fly—ozone-free light
that irradiates and warps the gene,
acid rain that burns the feather,

and stinging air from great cities
that makes them fly blind. Storms
roll them into airy heaps, and guns
wink from estuary and pond
where they think to rest

until the beloved's wings go limp
and plummet to waiting teeth
happy to sink into grief. Only then
do the warm waters of their refuges
embrace and solace them

as they fall from the sky like confetti.
Are they so dumb or so forgetful
they come and come again each year
never changing their way?
Or from some well of fellow-feeling

do they forgive without demure
the death we bring as the one
the world exacts for life?
How innocent they are of our denials,
our artilleries of self-hatred and despair

that turn outward and become bullet and gun.
The sun shimmers from spread wings,
their cries and scribbles crowd the sky—
then they are gone, as though erased,
a last feather spiraling down

through the silencing, haunted air.

WHAT GOD DOES WITH OWLS

Have you seen an owl die? Or
are they the true immortals, feeding
on the carelessness of others?
Maybe their bodies incandesce
at the moment of death
like a camera's white flash…

Does God give them then a place
on the tree of life, in heaven, never
to hunt the small shapes at its base?
Or does He put them in
some dark corner of His mind
where every hunt succeeds,

meat a hot, perfect red,
nights full of small scurryings,
thuds, sudden cut-off screams?
And does He who is everywhere
loose Himself through the air
in them too, talons out-stretched,

deal the deadly blow, tear a cry
with his yellow beak, stretch out
his head to let warm flesh slide
down his maw, enthralled
while a heart still beats in His claws?
What does He do with owls?

Surely not condemn them for doing
what He made them for?
I think they are closer to His heart
than us, like all wild things, because
they are perfect in their wills,
in their griefs, their pleasures—

not cross-grained with defiance
like ourselves, careworn, at a loss
to make sense of Him, or our lives.
It is us He puts in some dark corner
so we cannot infect these others
with our wear, and doubt, and wonder.

PERRY MILL POND

I am the enemy here
as grey clouds hold their breath.
Squirrels run through the trees'
green alcoves bordering the shore,
loosening small rainfalls
onto the pond: wood ducks
explode to flight, then herons
lurch loose-limbed across
the unfurled bolt of silk
carelessly left out to soak.
Mill, dam and wheel turned
by the waters' pent churn are gone,
hunters barred, this earth restored
to marginal wildness,
but memory of the death we bring
is bred in the bones of these that fly
however I want to dance
with quick feet in the leaves
or snap gunshot wings
or beat slow as calm breath
over marred landscapes
in search of some place free
of even the memory of old violence.

AN OLD BARN IN WESTON

stands in a field of dandelions blooming
so intensely the sky steals their hue.
A few tools rust, abandoned; the lofts sag,
barely able to support their emptiness,
and the barren stalls lose even the memory
of horse and cow or crowing barnyard fowl.
Homes fill once wheat-rich fields,
bound by law to look older than they are:
metal snakes commute down Lyons Plains Road
each morning, and each evening, home:
by day lonely women lug their wetnosed young
chore to chore or, chauffeurs by night,
drive young couples date to date
who all but couple in the backseat dark.
No matter. A trunk weathered white holds
the barn gates closed: heat warps the walls
that ice cracks in turn. If time speeded
the stained brown walls would hurry inward
under the falling roof, groaning with relief.
No one comes here now except barn mouse
and field, who was always here, and,
ghosting on wide wings as twilight falls,
great white mouse-harrowing owls.

ANGELS

His death is so new blood smokes into the colored air
    the screen places in my living room.
A woman bends over him, arms thrown wide then folded
    over her breast,
repeating all the crucial gestures of those medieval figures
painted at the foot of Christ's cross as the body descends.

Younger, I watched the city burn while I lounged in a pool,
only later learning Watts was smoking picturesquely
    in the distance.
I felt divorced from my own distress.
Now I become the woman and kneel by the curb,

a babble of Spanish grief on my lips:
I crane past the police cordon, too,
                      an onlooker eating
blood and lamentation. Only moments ago
the gun trembled in my hands like a woman in ecstasy.
The soul can be anything

a life grows into its care.
Being human is an ideal, something akin to a painted
    angel on blue or gold
just out of reach of earthly hands.
I shut the image off and the screen, luminous and virginal,
dims slowly into the darkness where I am.

BORDER CROSSING

On the beach south of Ensenada
the pelican-threaded surf
through wavecrash and foamrun
and the groaning suck home says
"nothing nothing, nothing:"

far to the north at Big Sur the same
white words. Between these Mexicans
stand on a wave of land in Tijuana,
reduced to silhouettes by brutal
border lights—they look like trees

after a fire has swept them,
hoping to slip in a confused
moment into that brilliant land.
I feel their hunger as I pass, the
commonplace heartlessness

of men set against men,
the pity in my heart that leads
to nothing but waste blood,
a black thread in the dark red.
There are friends to think of,

the drug of easy pleasures:
I put these others from mind
until the surf takes on urgency
when the house sleeps. Then
I see them stripped by desire

to outlines of humanity, men
who want what they cannot have
and despise what they do. Men
like me. Mile after mile the
white words tumble on the beach.

MADONNAS AND OTHER STRANGERS

A child is found when the watchman sees
a light in a high, abandoned room
and thuds upwards, breathing heavily,
to where he thinks the squatters are
but finds in that squalid place a dead newborn
who glows, a small sun, though cold,
and stiller than bare bone—
> *no, the girl-child lives,*
> *her light holds the rats at bay,*
> *fading only in his calloused hands.*

Every night he peers into lives pale as his own,
and draws small reassurance there—
he cannot forget what dimmed in his grasp.
Troubled, anxious, soon he thinks
it was a only a dream or some
confused memory from his youth.

He tells his wife nothing over tea,
only stares at the crimson islands lips and nails
make on her white skin, and feels such uneasiness
he cannot eat. His darts fly astray at the pub,
but he tells his mates nothing, aghast
how only bitters rouge their cheeks.

Now when the late sun or later streetlights
touch high abandoned windows,
or when the eyes of a woman shine too brightly,
he sees that glow again, and knows
men consume that fire

*as one will his daughter
who hopes in terror and hunger
in the high room of her loneliness
to lure some man with her own radiance.
Then, drained, she will haunt his hunger too
as he stares past her polishes and creams
into those white surfaces that mirror his own.*

PIAF SINGS

over scandals couples share
between bites as dishes
and silverware scrape,

Piaf decades dead
whom I don't understand
except for her passion

we treat here as atmosphere.

But the heart knows its music
across time, against death,
the heart so like but unlike

the whale so small in the sea
that fills a great depth
with aching songs.

Her passion islands me

among these strangers until
I lift my voice with hers—
then silence falls, amazed.

My food grows cold, and I feel
well up from the ground the
great yearning of earth and stone

for the little lives we waste.

VENUS AT VERDUN

We change, but not in sacred eyes
where time is one swollen moment,
a prism turned in history's light
where tourists babble in the tunnels
as soldiers use their bayonets to scramble
each others' bowels, and French and German
vowels blend in a common scream
as children beg for sodas and ice cream.

Outside men go down in long rows
like wheat scythed by a hissing blade
in fields cratered and bare—and
newly sheeted with poppies and grass
where they follow their guide in single file.
She sees new soldiers make love
sensing death in the room—
and nuzzle, newborn, their mother's breasts

who cannot see the tangled ground
where they fall and freeze, or mushroom
in August heat below bomb-burst skies,
but feel it in their tears and blood and bones
as families search from white cross
to cross under the summer sun.
What can Venus say?
She aches for love, to take these men

in her arms and give them
her little death for the greater,
murmuring, impassioned, *Forget, forget*—
but knows tragedy and joy make one whole.
Here a man fishes the Meuse

stripped of cover and densely treed,
his rod ticking death all one afternoon
to fish he piles agleam and agape

in a golden gas of sunlight—
and leaden as the bomb fragments
raining down, like the twigs
a father and daughter throw from the bridge,
then race to the other side to see
whose floats by first, and wins,
in water that in Venus' violet eyes is
so slow and green, and streaming red.

DRIVING INTO ITALY

Slathered by rain, shaken by thunder
I never see german cupolas give way
to campaniles. But once past Verona
     another world
         another sun
colors so infused with light
even the dried fields of sunflowers
are just fallen ash, and still burn invisibly.
Pure hues of green and yellow shoot sunward,
and the tiled farmhouse roofs, and their
decayed gold and brown stucco walls,
echo the burnt sienna of new-plowed fields.
When I stop, light floods out of our faces,
and goes through my outspread hands—
I feel bright as Adam on his first afternoon
before confusion twined with the sweat and
     strain of living
to make him fully human.

         Oh, I know
how bloodsoaked this earth is—a fort,
chapel and monastery on every hill,
churches common as loaves in the cities:
every inch of land claimed from a
savagery and belief in flesh so intense
two thousand years leave the work undone,
the body counts on my own streets
nothing to those stuffed in the earth, here...

But this light makes me briefly
new as a child in his new world...
That glow lasts while I go on driving,

it hardly matters where, so long
as I have never been there before
and can forget how the film of years
has dulled my skin, and wisdom deepened
as I have grown manly and corrupt.

RAPALLO

Who cares
    the stucco flakes and fades
from pediments, columns,
    carved bases painted
around the windows and
    even in alleys or
apartments facing rails?
    Figures of angels are
frozen in flight, or Mary
    sad in bright colors;
friezes of saints or gods
    circle the roofs; facades
of faux masonry vary
    with baroque flourishes
around plain doors:
    dead ends become
passages to ideal streets
    we vainly hunger for.
Do those within feel
    equal to the grandeur
spent so casually elsewhere
    by turning all to ornament?
mocking faiths
    that died, the freedom
come and gone and come
    again, blood flowing
in the streets, or peace
    dozing through rumors
of great events in summer's
    sun or by a winter's fire?
Or do they preserve
    these changes lightly,

keeping images of
    each transcended
near as family photos
    on the bureau,
some yellowed, some
    just framed, so generous
they include those
    who argued more
than loved?
    This place shows
my own ambiguity
    to age, a puzzle of
acceptance and disguise,
    a reminder though I
once insisted all
    be what they seemed,
the years have planted
    multitudes in my heart
whose only claim to
    harmony or sense is
they are who I am.
    I am in Rapallo now
wherever I go,
    haunted by the thought
the ideal place
    I cannot find
is what I blindly live
    confused or sorrowing
one piece at a time.

THE LIGHT AT RAPALLO

is fine steel folded and beaten
until it forms a blade so
sharp and strong and bright
it blinds unless water
mediates its shine;

a child's 'O' of amazement

when a circus elephant rolls
on command or a tiger
holds a head harmless
in brilliant teeth;
a shooting star

in dim night skies,

a narwhale's white horn
in green waves,
a mirage whose brilliance deceives
because this light that lasts like iron
is soft.

In storms its beams

bore holes to the sea
or reflect from steaming promenades:
when black clouds swallow it whole,
they glow like flesh
lit from within,

while in hills where villas ride

like seagulls, waves
it touches the secret places of mushrooms
with a boar's white tusk—
only the heart knows a darkness
it cannot reach.

But this light is careless

whether we are here or
have killed ourselves—
its beauty is
a blade no one can wear,
a tiger no one can tame:

a tooth free of hunger.

DACHAU

I pour over maps in flight to a wedding
until, just north of Munich, I see   Dachau.
History is a dream in Los Angeles, but there
I could stroll barracks and ovens as though
      on any Sunday outing.

Both german and jew stir in my heart—
when my fathers abandoned history for America
      a century and more ago,
they left whole families behind to devour each other:
perhaps one forbear casually flipped the switch
      releasing gas,
while another shipped in from Kiev or Vilna
      beat the air and cried
as the showerheads shook and hissed…

The same skill in killing turns now towards
      ruthless comfort:
if, tired, I fell in Munich's new airport, a bed
placed just so after careful calculation
      would break my fall,
while the roads south steer the car as though
      trapped within a map.
Then a surprise—pastoral as Iowa, green
      as Vermont,
the air a familiar, humid flood,
the landscape brings no comfort but tells me
even here I am less a stranger than I thought.

In Italy as my daughter treads the aisle amid
      our jubilation,
and her child wails, full of new life, I go on

    awakening to Dachau's life—
and how both killer and sufferer root equally
       in my blood.

HISTORY

Sometimes history is a woman
at the far end of a crowded coach
with a swan's neck and breast
and a Hollywood ingenue's profile,
a woman who always has just made love.

I catch her eye, and she surprises
by moving beside me aglow, scented with sex,
then takes me off to St. Martin-in-the-Fields
where once clergy fed the hungry
but now the affluent dine above

the gravestones of the faithless dead.
She stops at the stalls where Russians sell
the Revolution and Great War—busts
of Lenin and Stalin, medals, awards—
whole lives, profound valor,

and cruelty beyond the byzantine
reduced to costume jewelry—
and has me pin a red star on her breast.
She admires herself with a laugh,
brushes my cheek with her lips, and vanishes.

Her perfume lingers in the air,
and I feel her eyes pass over me
from behind the rows of batiked dresses
that droop like the banners of some great knight
as once must have gone by here before

she turned him into tapestry and decor.
I am worth no more than this tease,
a common man who escapes her fixed stare,
glad to be a plain thread in her weave,
not golden, not red.

END OF THE CENTURY

The center starts to hold, and the beast withdraws
to the fringe with many a backward snap.
No shining figure drives him toward
his four-chambered lair that resounds with
red thunders and blind lightnings
from where he came so many years ago—

he retreats to distant fields because he drove *us* past
    exhausted violence to boredom.
The hollow dead, million-mouthed, remind us
he is the tooth in our blood and claw in our bone,

and though we reproach the stars,
or the god who made us,
long ages of violence have taught
we caress then ravage all we love.
But for now doves with wings tipped red
replace his guardian vultures and crows;

great cities clean his slime, and gleam:
we dream of faith, of good works to make us whole,
of strange translations of machine to man

or man to star-bound, metal voyager
taking our tale to alien, astonished ears.
We grow blithe, and hope for private edens,
as though history is done or what rests in the heart
will not emerge with a newborn, killing beauty
when we tire of doves and call him again,
    firmly,
        Come!

THE QUAKER GRAVEYARD IN NANTUCKET

They baffle me, these nonviolent men
who still heave harpoons in their dreams
at peaceful islands of flesh, then stitch
through ribs with long spears until
they stab the heart and spumes of blood
rain on their sober grey, man and whale
wallowing in a sea stained red.
Still they flench flail slice hook drop
the whale's flesh in boiling pots,
refining all anguish and triumph
to an oil they sell at premium prices
to other men they never would harm
or help. Their wives beside them dream
of store openings, of cash and flow
to mark the days before, oil-smeared and reeking,
their men come home to spawn in them,
and later in their maids: such ecstasies
rained from attic rooms and cupolas…

When these Quakers gathered in church,
they struck through silence to God,
spearing Him with such passion
man and woman sweated tears
that ran down their cheeks, so transported
they changed sorrow and pain to delight,
and evil, grained in the world like quartz
in softer stone, to clay.
          They knew
right turns wrong with the flip of a fluke,
that the heart is flat deep cut whole rank

lustrous.
    So they forgave Friend Owen Chase
who ate his men to survive the long row
to Chile after the whale sank the Essex,
not a make-believe Ahab but one of their own
who found the human and inhuman
lie close in a man's heart.

Night opens and closes overhead;
thunder and unrolling, strobe-lit silks
trail eastward over the waters:
stars tirelessly dry the darkness.
The Quakers sheathe their spears
and guide grave ships over swells
I cannot see, their wives patient
as when fog rolled in morning and night,
so fused with sunlight they were blinded,
and thought the strange hard husbands
forming before them were black,
imagined shapes. Now, a jet ride away
the grave Pacific rolls over
wreck and tooth-scored bone:
nearer, hasty, the careless Atlantic
bares a keel on a sunken bank,
then covers both once more—while in town
all have forgotten how a hand may slice
an innocent heart, yet still caress so
even reluctant knees buckle and fold...

Let me not feel small beside these men,
ashamed at the gentle mercy lavished on my life
that finds no evil without repair
or grief without recovery.
Let me not grieve for murder at sea

or lust by land, or the hard inner light
that holds all conflict within one sphere
and sees true—
        for my innocence slips
under their wake as a whale's stripped body,
cut loose from the head, drifts down
to the depths where evil abides, and courage,
and lust, and the sea's violent peace.

WHY THE WOMAN LIGHTHOUSE KEEPER STAYS AT POINT PINOS

1

The light burning into the dying
eyes of sailors as they go down
to their drenched holocaust, cursing,
lives in the tower's tooth behind the beach
where the beast of the foghorn lows all night.
When my children call from their dreams
in fear of the wet ship of the ocean
with its dreadful cargo
I soothe their sleep with lies:
    "Hush, darling, you hear nothing" or
    "No, no darling, there is nothing to see"
for the drowned men are bells,
and ring among the sunken ships;
the drowned men are lights
and shine in the depths
where hunters angle their own bright flesh
    for prey.
Some nights, when the moon wears a shroud
they pool together in phosphorescent schools—
the fishermen know when they spill
nothing from their drenched nets—
only the mesh gleams
until rinsed again in the sea.

2

One calm, clouded night I went to the shore
the wind still, and the waves,

even the foghorn, broken:
only the light turning and turning behind me

like meat on a spit
swept over the sea

as though beckoning.
The small lights of the drowned converged

until a broad beam lapped the shore—
when I touched that brilliance,

it clothed me, I shone
as though on fire.

> they said *We are changed, not dead
> though dead to you, moving
> steadily in the sea's steep currents.
> We hate your heat, the terrible
> briefness of your purpose;
> hate the living heave of
> your belly and the greedy thirst
> of your thighs; hate
> that light behind you
> rolling horizons together, as if worlds
> and time and hunger were cheap
> and they are.
>   Come, be
> distilled to us—*

*all that holds us
even this close to life is your grief.
We hate that most.*

3

When at length I fall asleep
near my children who rest
like infants on the breast

once primal fear has worn them down
and peace curls and settles
on their brows,

I know something bred in the bone
hates life
and even then is eager to be free.

That hatred is our mystery,
something we must teach to forgive and remember
that we may live despite our pain.

So you will find my spirit here,
mourning,
as anyone must who loves,

long after the point is stripped
of cypress and pine to fuel
the local fires. Hear me

in the sea lions' roars,
in the foghorn and ocean breaking
on land and rock in wind and fog—

or see me, though all slips away
and so much so willingly,
in that great wheel of light

rolling our darkness home.

THE FRUIT TREES AT GUNNERS-
BURY CEMETERY

for Jeanne: in memoriam
 Violet Cresswell

What a wildness of blossoms and bees
roots here in hard death and rules
over loss, or those puzzled
who feel none. Petals dust effigies

pounded in autumn by falling fruit,
while today April mixes with August
heat and light and stuns the
new queens flying ripe with young.

Dark jackets drop from old shoulders
like leaves clinging to winter's limbs:
crewcut, freckled, stolid, red,
the Church of England man delivers

the last words with the reverence of a
long-haul driver for the straightest route
between pickup and drop-off, then mops
his brow as we toss down handfuls of earth.

Sweet Violet, few cry for you
in this small cortege of faithless lovers,
friends, remnant family once so large,
that trailed your hearse to hollowed ground.

Though Grandmother Cresswell lies near,
her one son at her feet, his in turn
stands bemused as the rest,
for these in their bare English way

who live so close to each other
prefer to be in memory than communion.
Only the distant woman in America
death makes a child again, sobs,

for you were my wife's true mother
as her own hurried from
man to man during the war
to make half-unknown half sisters—

then abandoned all. As we turn to go
invisible vultures flap towards your flat
where kin and in-law will paw your goods
and sell your remnants to each other—

I will rifle boxes of billet doux,
and find a photo of the man
who jilted you lying on your
unused trousseau: even

the great piano in the parlor
that pushed us into corners, unplayed
for decades, will swing out the window
for three hundred pounds, groaning.

Some autumn I will return when wind
tosses fruit on the ground and frost
sweetens those left on the limb.
Are they apple—Winesap, Redstrake,

Golden to judge beauty? Ashfull
Sodom? Are they pear, Elberta, sweet
Comice; Wolf? Or plum, Sugar and
Blood, or Wild? Peach, clingstone,

free, downy as velvet? Or just
plain local Gunnersbury Quince?
No matter...
      I will pluck one then,
my tongue crush the sweet pulp—

the sun will reel, mourners frown—
for this is the fruit forbidden us
that looses death's grip, full of the
starstuff in every atom's core

that builds each Adam's life.
Its meat is bitter, and teaches
how we come and come again
no matter what dissolvings

of the single mind, or frostings
of our skins, or swift uprushes
of the hard but readied ground:
of how something works through us

towards greater life—or fills its time
with our mere, mindless striving.
What sense I shape from this
must grow and die with myself:

hived even in bittersweet lines,
we believe only what we live.
For now, at least, I take my leave.
The gates go out of focus

as I drive away, while the light
enjoys a mysterious hour alone
as blue burns to white, then grey.
I tell all this to the woman

gentle as her aunt. Now composed,
she touches the unused bridal silks
half in wonder, half with that reverence
love brings to mere things—

and I see, suddenly, how we add
to who we are and what we mean
no matter the surrounding emptiness
by just such small increments of love

we are too simple to withhold
and defiant to forget:
of how, invisibly, something new
grows step by step.

DUST

Sheets balled or blown wide
stream up the cliff and
shred on the ridge
as bright drops splash
on the path, sieved from
a green mesh of cypresses.
No warning reaches the trawler

homing too near the shore—

this fog shrouds the lighthouse
and blows the horn inland.
A tear in the gray, surf flaring,
the beam suddenly overhead,
and the boat drops on rocks
reefed out from the headland—
only the great-eyed sea lions

skirting the line of danger

see the crates, nets, buoys
orange life jackets, flashes
of silver bodies shattered
free from the hold
smash against the cliff,
and the current running here
suck down the men

and bear them off.

Was God here when they died?
> *He is everywhere.*
Why not lift His hand
against the wave, then?

He cannot care
> *He cares*
or have the power to prevent
> *He does*
then the will to forbear

from adding to our suffering.
> *Power spurs him*
> *to do what can be done.*

Does He forget all power
meets greater, and with one
great O of wonder goes down
like these men in the brutal surge?
> *He must do what can be done*
> *whatever that is, because it can.*

The newborn's cry in the ward
a floor below where the
comatose die, the rain

of ashen flesh always falling
in some Dachau of His mind,
the first true kiss of a virgin
who discovers flesh is fire?
> *He is all, and was born,*
> *and must die, in fire*

> *or such dispersion as one sees*

    only in drowned mens' eyes.
Is it pity, then, He needs?

    No: power must be used
    or lost. He must ride
    or be ridden, and though
    the rowels in His sides are razors,
    He cannot outrace Himself.
A man might think of mercy, then.

* * *

A quick, hot ray warms me

through a break in the fog,
and resined freshness lifts
from the cypresses: my mind
drifts to dreamless sleep.
Simple pleasures, fully savored,

swiftly gone, not beyond hope

of renewal, become my goal—
wisdom I despised for accepting evil
when I thought change possible
instead of endless recurrence,
that I could tame the fierce beasts

that people my heart, even

the snake coiled at the brain's base—
but the genes thread our character
no less than His on iron rails,
while great nets tirelessly
sieve our tears from the

wind of our unknowing.

As I grow older, and plainer,
I think of this dust I am:
each atom was forged in a star,
each combined and recombined
until I could question

fruitlessly, what we are for.

But now the way
common things turn revelatory
tugs at my mind—
how the bleak, long grass
of late summer turns

in an angle of light

to goldsmith's work,
filigreed and gleaming,
how then even the dust
blazes with beauty,
and does not ask why,

or whether, or for justice,

but burns down death's
long fuse into life.
Suddenly I wonder
how else could it be?
and turn towards that wisdom.

I burn with its hunger.

INNOCENCE

Spare shafts of sunlight hallow common things
    for lucky men,
a swing, say, hung from an old rafter
that shakes the barn with all of childhood when
    swung,
or the rafter itself, hallowed by use,
or two apples that fall from a bowl into the light
    of memory
where they are restored by worn, loved hands.
For others, things are water in their grasp, unable
to slake the hunger for root, earth, lip,
the deep-thrust, well-worn, often kissed that make
    the known, rare.

What has saved me, born with a silver spoon in
    my mouth?
Let me find the sacred in fresh sawn wood, its dust
    sweet as new mown hay
but without its bitter undertaste of decay;
in light on the meadow, cloud on the mountain,
spring seawater numbing my feet, the noon blaze
    gilding spartina?
In the sweet inner run of a woman's thigh,
and sweeter vulva from where we blink into
    light?

By instinct, or just luck—and a taste for the same
things and others over and over like a child,
the constant reuse of ourselves by ourselves dissolving
    I/Thou into one self;
by that innocence not given, not earned, not young or
    old, and

baffling the adult, ambivalent mind, not lost,
but always there like dull stones on a path
stray shafts of sunlight burn gold.

WOLF WIND

I know where blood, hand, cry, bone, pleasure, grief, stone
flare and fade like the ghost particles that fill empty space
    with their hunger to be,
teasing as if memory's dream in a memory held in dream.

When I think
    This is the best my life can be
the wind blowing from there whispers
    Every joy is shadow and soon done;
    not even loss stays to anchor you in the real.
Contempt of flesh or exile from all that makes life precious
    give no shield:
this wind feeds on the common fear that makes all men one.

Deep in the woods it fans the fire that torches the tallest tree
    and chars all life—
yet new lives open from seeds
when downpours spill from mouths
only fire makes smile—
the fuse that burns up the root
knows this wind as the bright mother from whom it comes.

I might call it love, but that seems too hard or too wide
or too far from our own that wants to hold and hold
    and teach time to let go.
Let it stay nameless, then, not even God:
despair and solace, it is the terrible beauty that blows through everything.

THE SOUTH SUSSEX DOWNS

Everywhere the ancestral mind—
field, windbreak, barrow, altar: on the crests
warriors and horses etched in chalk
refuse to go away, like bad dreams.
Everywhere the ancestral wind, blue and silver—
Mary's colors, the mother the pilgrims loved
who once traced this road through Alfriston,
then abandoned with the dreams in chalk.
Light wheels across the shore-hugging sea:
rain falls with a thousand years' despair
and the downs hood their heads with dark mists

and then the amazing thing
the land takes itself back from us

swallowing every human sign except
the drunken will-o-the-wisp villages
that stumble in their muddy troughs.
"Can you feel the brooding?" asks my friend,
yes! I want to say, but I can't shake the terror
gripping my throat and then, huge,
the exhilaration:

> *as though*
> *I rise from a trance on the hill, set free*
> *by the land's freedom, made fully human*
> *only by passing through.*